Who Am I...Really?

Loveland, Colorado

Group's R.E.A.L. Guarantee to you:

This Group resource incorporates our R.E.A.L. approach to ministry—one that encourages long-term retention and life transformation. It's ministry that's:

Relational
Because learner-to-learner interaction enhances learning and builds Christian friendships.

Experiential
Because what learners experience through discussion and action sticks with them up to 9 times longer than what they simply hear or read.

Applicable
Because the aim of Christian education is to equip learners to be both hearers and doers of God's Word.

Learner-based
Because learners understand and retain more when the learning process takes into consideration how they learn best.

Note:
The price of this text includes the right for you to make as many copies of the studies as you need for your immediate church group. If another church or organization wants copies of these studies, it must purchase *Christian Character Development Series: Who Am I...Really?* for its own use.

Christian Character Development Series: Who Am I...Really?

Copyright © 2000 and 2002 Group Publishing, Inc.

2002 edition

All rights reserved. No part of this book may be reproduced in any manner whatsoever without prior written permission from the publisher, except where noted in the text and in the case of brief quotations embodied in critical articles and reviews. For information, write Permissions, Group Publishing, Inc., Dept. PD, P.O. Box 481, Loveland, CO 80539.

Visit our Web site: www.grouppublishing.com

Credits

Contributing Authors: Mikal Keefer, Julie Meiklejohn, Siv M. Ricketts, Tim and Alison Simpson, and Jane Vogel
Book Acquisitions Editor: Julie Meiklejohn
Editor: Debbie Gowensmith
Creative Development Editor: Dave Thornton
Chief Creative Officer: Joani Schultz
Copy Editor: Stephen Beal
Art Director: Kari K. Monson
Cover Art Director: Jeff A. Storm
Computer Graphic Artist: Pat Miller
Cover Designer and Artist: Alan Furst, Inc. Art and Design
Illustrator: Amy Bryant and Matt Wood
Production Manager: Peggy Naylor

Unless otherwise noted, Scripture taken from the HOLY BIBLE, NEW INTERNATIONAL VERSION®. Copyright © 1973, 1978, 1984 by International Bible Society. Used by permission of Zondervan Publishing House. All rights reserved.

ISBN 0-7644-2428-9
10 9 8 7 6 5 4 3 2 1   11 10 09 08 07 06 05 04 03 02
Printed in Canada.

Contents

Introduction 4

How to Use This Book 4

Other Topics 6

The Studies

    1. A Place to Belong 7
            We're all important members of the family of God.

    2. Wanna Play Dress Up? 16
            God wants us to live righteous lives.

    3. Getting to Give 23
            Spiritual gifts come from God and are to be
            used to build up the church and glorify God.

    4. Who Am I? 30
            Our self-esteem comes from God.

    5. The Making of a Hero 36
            Christ is our one true hero.

    6. It's Who You Are That Counts 44
            God wants us to focus on him rather than on being popular.

    7. True Success 52
            True success comes from surrendering our lives to God.

    8. One Step at a Time 57
            We can trust God to guide our future.

Introduction

Our teenagers may be talking the talk, but are they walking the walk? Often an enormous gap exists between the Christian values many teenagers claim to have and their actions. Take a moment to ponder these sobering statistics:

- Six out of ten Christian teens say there is no such thing as absolute truth.

- One out of four deny the notion that acting in disobedience to God's laws brings about negative consequences.

- One-half believe the main purpose of life is enjoyment and personal fulfillment.

- Almost half contend that sometimes lying is necessary.

What's wrong with this picture?

Today's teenagers face more choices than any teenagers before them have. They are asked to interpret, evaluate, and make moral decisions within a culture that ignores morality and changes rapidly. The choices your teenagers make today have eternal consequences. Can their faith keep up?

How can we help? We can begin by taking them on a journey—a journey toward stronger, more Christlike character. As teenagers learn to interpret and evaluate their decisions in light of their relationships with God, they will discover the importance of living out their faith in everything they do.

How to Use This Book

Who Am I...Really? contains eight studies, each designed to address an aspect of students' emerging identities, and help them live out their spiritual lives.

- The study about **the family of God** helps students understand that they and other Christians are important members of God's family.

- The study about **righteousness** defines righteousness as becoming more like Christ and contrasts the slavery to sin with slavery to God.

- In the study about **spiritual gifts**, students discover that each Christian has an indispensable role to fill as part of Christ's body.

- In the study about **self-esteem**, students learn that God loves them as his children, a fact that can assure them of their importance and worth.

- The study about **role models and heroes** prompts students to think about the effect on their lives if they reacted to Christ as their one true hero.

- The study about **popularity** challenges students to re-evaluate the importance they put on being popular and encourages them to strive toward Christlike behavior.

- The study about **success** urges students to turn the microscope on themselves to evaluate how striving for worldly success prevents them from surrendering their lives to God.

- In the study about **the future**, students discover what it means to them that God will guide them, one step at a time, throughout the present and future.

The *Christian Character Development Series* encourages students to examine their own character in a very individual, personal way. Each study in this series guides students to examine the topic individually, in pairs, and in larger groups.

Each study connects the topic and the Scriptures to God-centered character development—the idea that God gives us a model of quality character in his Word, as well as a desire to know him and to become more like him.

Before each study, photocopy the entire study for each person. Each person in your group will have his or her own set of handouts to use extensively throughout each study for journaling and other writing and drawing activities. Each study begins with a section called "Read About It" and then follows with a section called "Write About It." These sections provide teenagers with "food for thought" about the topic and provide the opportunity to respond to those thoughts, right on their papers. You may choose to have your students complete these sections before your group meets, or you may decide to have students complete these sections at the beginning of your meeting time.

Other sections of the study are designed so students can work through them with a minimum of direction from you. Any direction you may need to give your students is included in the "Leaders Instructions" boxes. You're encouraged to participate and learn right along with the students—your insights will enhance students' learning.

Each study provides a combination of introspective, active, and interactive learning. Teenagers learn best by experiencing the topic they're learning about and then sharing their thoughts and reactions with others.

Christian Character Development Series: Who Am I...Really? will help you guide your teenagers through the perils and pitfalls of growing up in today's culture. Use the studies in this book to work with your youth to understand what it means to have high standards of character and to learn why character is important to God.

Other Topics

Who Am I With Others?
Knowing God
Conflict
Forgiveness
Friendships
Parents and Other Authorities
Dating
Loneliness
Love

Who Am I Inside?
Hope
Fear
Guilt
Pride
Joy
Grief
Anger
Peace

Who Am I to Judge?
Sex
Drugs and Alcohol
Peer Pressure
Moral Absolutes
Idolatry
Media and Music
Handling Stress
Making Good Decisions

Who Am I When Nobody's Looking?
Honesty
Wisdom
Integrity
Humility
Trust
Generosity
Compassion
Faithfulness

Who Am I to God?
Salvation
The Bible
The Trinity
Prayer
Service
Faith
Sharing Faith
Worship

A Place to Belong

 We're all important members of the family of God.

Supplies: You'll need Bibles, rubber bands, crayons, and pens.

Preparation: Set out the supplies on a table.

Leader Instructions

Begin by having students each read the "Read About It" section and respond in the "Write About It" section.

Read About It

It was just another day for a widow, another day of growing older alone. She drifted through the streets, unnoticed, mindful that nobody waited for her at home.

Part of a culture in which widows were without social status, she was also terribly poor. She knew that when she died, her body would be carried away, her very few possessions would be sold, and she would soon be forgotten.

So it wasn't surprising that no one at the Temple seemed to notice her as she shuffled across the crowded hall, reached into her pocket, drew out the coins, then dropped them into the box.

Two coins. It was all she had. A tiny offering from a forgotten old woman.

As a woman, she couldn't even enter certain parts of the Temple. As a widow, she was an uncomfortable reminder of death. As a pauper, she didn't merit any special consideration. Yet in the kingdom of God, she was a giant.

Write About It

Read Mark 12:41-43, and then respond to the following questions:

• How do you think this widow felt as she dropped her coins into the treasury?

A Place to Belong ♦ 7

- The widow was unaware of the impact she had on others. Who has had a positive influence on your life without realizing it?

- Describe someone you know who isn't all that impressive in the eyes of the world but who has been an example of God's kingdom to you.

- If you stopped the widow and asked her whether she considered herself an important member of God's family, how do you think she'd answer? Why? If she asked you the same question, how would you answer? Why?

Experience It

Leader Instructions

Have students form four groups, and point out the supply table you prepared before the study.

Follow the instructions on the "All in the Family" page (p. 9) in your group. Use the supplies on the supply table as needed.

Tell Me More...

"Yet to all who received him, to those who believed in his name, he gave the right to become children of God."

—John 1:12

All in the Family
Section 1

Imagine that the dinner bell at your house has rung and your family has come to dinner. In the box below, draw your family at dinner.

Read Luke 8:19-21 and Galatians 3:26-29. Now imagine that the dinner bell has rung again and God's family has come to dinner. In the box below, draw that family at dinner.

Share your sketches with your group members, discuss the following questions, and write your comments in the spaces provided.

- How does someone qualify to join the first family you drew?

- How does someone qualify to join God's family?

- How might you look at people differently if you thought of them as being part of your family through God?

- How might you look at yourself differently if you thought of yourself as being part of God's family?

Section 2

In the space below, write the following sentence: "There's nothing wrong with my writing."

_____

_____

Loop a rubber band several times around the little finger and middle finger of your writing hand. Connect those two fingers tightly enough to immobilize them, but not tightly enough to cut off circulation.

Now write, "There's nothing wrong with my writing" in the space below.

_____

_____

Remove the rubber band, discuss the following questions, and write your comments in the spaces provided.

- Read 1 Corinthians 12:12-13, 27. What does this Scripture tell you about the importance of the members of your youth group or church?

_____

- How did the "loss" of your fingers affect your writing? How is that like what happens when each member of God's family isn't seen as important?

_____

- How does the importance of everyone in God's family change the way you look at others? at yourself?

_____

Leader Instructions

Have everyone form a circle to read together 1 Corinthians 13:1-13. Explain that students will be passing a Bible around the circle and taking turns reading consecutive verses. If someone doesn't want to read aloud, that person should pass the Bible to the next person. Otherwise, a person should state the verse number he or she will read, read the verse, then pass on the Bible.

Have someone begin by reading 1 Corinthians 13:1. When the group has finished with verse 13, process the experience using questions such as these:

- How does it feel to belong to a family of love?
- How is our church a family of love? How does our church fall short of being a family of love?
- How is our group a family of love? How do we fall short of being a family of love?
- How do you bring love to God's family? How do you fall short of bringing love to God's family?
- Do you feel as if you belong in God's family? Why or why not?

Apply It

We all have trouble valuing certain people or groups of people. With those people, we're generally quicker to judge and slower to break down barriers. Complete the "Party Squares" page (p. 12) to examine who you have trouble valuing.

When you've finished the page, find a partner to compare party notes with. Summarize below the sort of person you are least likely to value by stringing together descriptions of those you'd be least likely to seek out at a party.

_____

_____

- Does anyone in God's family meet that description? Explain.

_____

- As a family member, what might be your responsibilities toward that person?

_____

With your partner, pray for someone you've dismissed as irrelevant or unimportant. Ask God for forgiveness and for opportunities to reach out.

Party Squares

Pretend you're attending a party at which there are seven rooms to explore. In each room, different groups of people are standing in the corners, talking. In each room, decide which corner you're most likely to gravitate toward and which corner you're least likely to gravitate toward. Try to respond honestly from your first impressions.

Write an L for "least likely" in the corner you'd be *least* likely to visit. Write an M for "most likely" in the corner you'd be *most* likely to visit.

1. In this room, people have formed groups by age.

Younger than 15	16 to 25
26 to 35	36 and older

2. In this room, people have formed groups by race.

White	Black
Asian	Hispanic

3. In this room, people have formed groups by marital status.

Single	Married
Divorced	Widowed

4. In this room, people have formed groups by political comfort zones.

Conservative	Liberal
Moderate	Indifferent

5. In this room, people have formed groups by education.

High school dropout	High school graduate
College graduate	College degree holder

6. In this room, people have formed groups by gender.

All male	All female
Mostly male	Mostly female

7. In this room, people have formed groups by special interests.

Sports	Science
Art	Politics

A Place to Belong ◆ 13

Live It

Interview two or three people from the family of God this week. Try to talk to people you may have accidentally dismissed in the past. Ask them the following questions or your own questions:

- What does it mean to you that you are an important part of a larger family, the family of God?

_____

_____

- How has the family of God made a difference in your life?

_____

_____

Have students each choose a potential member of God's family to get to know better, invite to youth group activities, and talk to about their faith.

- What do you consider to be the rights and responsibilities of members of God's family toward each other? toward those currently outside the family?

_____

_____

After completing the interviews, answer the questions for yourself. Then think of two things you can do to be an active, loving member of God's family. Write those two goals below.

_____

_____

Now pray, asking God to help you understand what it means to be a part of his family and to fulfill your commitments to his family.

Tell Me More...

It's tempting to think that Jesus considers everyone a child of God. But at no time did Jesus announce that all people get to be God's children simply because they are God's creations.

Jesus did teach, however, that each person is a *potential* child of God. The offer was open to people of all nations (Matthew 8:11), but faith in Christ is the essential condition (John 1:12; 3:16).

Wanna Play Dress Up?

 God wants us to live righteous lives.

Supplies: You'll need Bibles, pens or pencils, a three-foot length of yarn for each person, balloons, and markers.

Preparation: Set out the supplies on a table.

Leader Instructions

Begin by having students each read the "Read About It" section and respond in the "Write About It" section.

Read About It

In *The Joyful Christian*, C. S. Lewis talks about the process of becoming like Jesus. For Christians, this is a process that happens slowly, over time, as we welcome Christ's presence and work in our lives. This process is never complete until death, when we join Christ in heaven.

In the meantime, though, we have the wonderful privilege of approaching God as our Father. Lewis points out that the Lord's Prayer begins with the words "Our Father." He explains, "They mean, quite frankly, that you are putting yourself in the place of a son of God. To put it bluntly, you are *dressing up as Christ*."

Our Christian lives should be a constant quest to live up to that role. Even though we aren't like Jesus, we should strive to become more like him every day.

Write About It

- What does Lewis mean when he suggests you can "dress up as Christ"?

- Close your eyes for a moment and "dress up as Christ." How would your life be different if you did this regularly?

- Explain righteousness using an example from your own life or from the life of someone you know.

Experience It

Leader Instructions

Have students form groups of four, and point out the supply table you prepared before the study.

Assign two people in each group to complete the "Pharisees" section in the "Models of Righteousness" page and the other two people to complete the "Abraham" section.

For Section 3 of the "Models of Righteousness" page, you may need to help students tie their pieces of yarn. You may also consider reading aloud the list of actions for the whole group to complete at the same time.

Follow the instructions on the "Models of Righteousness" page (p. 18) in your pairs. Use the supplies on the supply table as needed.

Tell Me More…

Slavery is an ugly concept, and people rebel against the idea of being a slave to anything. But becoming a slave to God is different. People owning people degrades everyone, but choosing to submit to God benefits everyone.

Besides, God is not a wicked slave driver. He won't ask you do to anything he wasn't willing to do himself. God's standards of righteousness are not toilsome; instead, they represent ways that God looks out for your best interests.

Models of Righteousness

Section 1

With your partner, complete your assigned section of the chart below.

	The Pharisees Read Matthew 23:23-28.	**Abraham** Read Hebrews 11:8-12.
Summarize the Scripture.		
Does this character demonstrate righteousness? If so, how? If not, why not?		
What do you learn about righteousness from this example?		

When you've finished your section of the chart, join with the other pair in your group to share what you've learned. Then discuss with your group the questions below and write your answers in the spaces provided.

• Contrast the righteousness of the Pharisees to that of Abraham. How are they different?

• How does it seem that the characters viewed God? themselves? Explain.

• At this moment, are you more like the Pharisees or Abraham? Explain.

• Who would you rather be like? Why? What can you do about it?

Section 2

Read Ephesians 4:22-24. As a group, discuss the following questions, and write your answers in the space provided.

• Describe your "old self."

- Describe your "new self."

- What does this passage say about righteousness?

Individually, draw pictures in the two columns below to represent the old clothes God wants you to take off and the new clothes God wants you to put on.

"Old Self"	**"New Self"**

When everyone in your group has finished drawing, take turns sharing one thing from each of your columns. Then pray together for continued wisdom and strength to put off the old self and put on the new self.

Section 3

Use a piece of yarn to tie your ankles together, making the loops of the bow big enough for your wrists to fit through. Double knot the bow, then put your wrists through the loops.

Now try to complete each of the following actions:
- Give someone a pat on the back.
- Walk and talk with a friend.
- Do an act of service for someone in this room.
- Read a Bible verse to a friend.
- Exchange a high five with a friend who has shared something to be joyful about.
- Read Romans 6:16-23.

Now remain tied and discuss the following questions:

- How well were you able to complete these actions? Why?

- How was this effort like being a slave to sin?

- According to this passage, what are the results of being slaves to sin?

Now take turns untying another group member. When you've been untied, read Romans 6:22-23 to yourself.

Get a balloon from the supply table. Blow it up, tie it to your piece of yarn, then tie it to your wrist. Try again to do a couple of the actions from the list above. When you've finished, rejoin your small group, discuss the following questions, and write your answers in the spaces provided.

- How was performing the same actions different this time?

- How would living with this kind of "burden" feel different from living tied up?

- How was this activity like being a slave to God?

- How does being a slave to God relate to righteousness?

- How can you become righteous?

- Why would you want to be righteous?

Becoming God's slave may be a funny concept, but God promises good things as a result. Using a marker, write on your balloon some of the benefits of slavery to God. Keep this balloon attached to your wrist for the remainder of the lesson, then take it with you to remind you of what you've learned.

Apply It

Read Ephesians 6:10-18 with your group, and then use the illustration below to follow these instructions:

- Label the parts of armor mentioned in the Scripture.
- Write one or two ways each piece of armor can help you to be righteous.
- At the bottom of the page, individually write a commitment to righteous living for this week.

Consider providing costumes for students to wear during this activity. The costumes can be as elaborate or as simple as you like. Remember to bring a camera and film, because you're sure to have some great photo opportunities. Debrief with questions such as these:
- Did wearing different clothes make you feel different? Explain.
- How is righteousness like a costume? How is it different?

Live It

Rate your righteousness on a scale of one to ten (ten is high). Explain why you chose that rating.

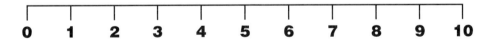

Use a concordance or Bible dictionary to learn more about righteousness. Look up passages dealing with righteousness, and ask yourself these questions:

- What does this passage say about righteousness?

Add fun and festivity to this lesson by using helium-filled balloons. They also may better communicate the "lightness" of God's "burden."

Wanna Play Dress Up? ◆ **21**

- How can I use what I've learned to live righteously every day?

Tell Me More...

God wants you to live a righteous life, but what happens if you blow it? God forgives, but confession is an important part of your relationship with God. When you hurt a friend, you have to admit that you did wrong in order for the relationship to continue and grow. It's the same with God. Even though you still have a relationship with him, you have to confess the sin in order receive forgiveness and maintain a healthy relationship.

And God is faithful. Psalm 130:3-4 promises that God doesn't keep a record of our sins. When God forgives them, they're gone.

Getting to Give

✝ **Spiritual gifts come from God and are to be used to build up the church and glorify God.**

Supplies: You'll need Bibles, pens or pencils, and a bag of individually wrapped candies.

Leader Instructions

Before teaching this lesson, review your church's beliefs about spiritual gifts. If you're not sure what your church teaches, check with your pastor or another church leader. Then adapt this lesson as needed to fit your church doctrine.

Leader Instructions

Begin by having students each read the "Read About It" section and respond in the "Write About It" section.

Read About It

Spiritual Gift*	Definition
Administration (1 Corinthians 12:28)	The ability to plan and oversee ministry operations.
Apostleship (1 Corinthians 12:28-29)	The ability to establish new ministries.
Discernment (1 Corinthians 12:10)	The ability to tell right from wrong.
Faith (1 Corinthians 12:9)	The ability to trust God and act accordingly.
Healing (1 Corinthians 12:9, 28, 30)	The ability to heal others physically or otherwise.
Helps (1 Corinthians 12:28)	The ability to provide support behind the scenes.
Interpretation (1 Corinthians 12:10)	The ability to understand and interpret when someone speaks in tongues.

(continued on the next page)

Spiritual Gift* (con't)	Definition (con't)
Knowledge (1 Corinthians 12:8)	The ability to understand and share God's truth.
Miracles (1 Corinthians 12:10, 28-29)	The ability to supernaturally show God's power.
Prophecy (1 Corinthians 12:10, 28)	The ability to speak God's truth.
Speaking in Tongues (1 Corinthians 12:10, 28-30)	The ability to speak in an unknown language.
Teaching (1 Corinthians 12:28-29)	The ability to teach God's truth to others.

*This list of spiritual gifts is not exhaustive and is based only on one passage of Scripture: 1 Corinthians 12:8-30.

Write About It

- Read John 14:16-17 and 1 Corinthians 12:7-11. Who has the Holy Spirit, and what does the Spirit do for them?

_____

_____

- Does the Spirit live in you? How do you know?

_____

_____

- Follow these directions:

Put a question mark by any gifts listed in the chart that you don't understand.

Put an exclamation point by gifts that sound exciting to you.

Put an X by gifts you've seen demonstrated.

Put a plus sign by gifts you think you might have.

Put a minus sign by gifts you think you don't have.

Experience It

Leader Instructions

Have students form groups of four, and point out the supply table you prepared before the study.

For Section 1 of the "Grace Gifts" page, assign two people in each group to read Romans 12:4-8; assign the other two to read Ephesians 4:4-6, 11-13.

When students are ready to begin Section 2 of the "Grace Gifts" page, give each student one, two, or five candies. Students can elect to do an act of service to earn another piece of candy, but they cannot earn more pieces of candy than you gave them at the beginning. For example, a person with three pieces of candy can do three acts of service to earn three more pieces of candy. After six minutes or when students appear to have finished, have them return to their groups.

Follow the instructions on the "Grace Gifts" page (p. 26) in your group.

Grace Gifts
Section 1

With your partner, read the passage you were assigned—either Romans 12:4-8 or Ephesians 4:4-6, 11-13—discuss the questions that follow, and write your answers in the spaces provided.

Read Romans 12:4-8.

- Why does the Spirit give gifts?

- How should people use their spiritual gifts?

- What does this passage tell you about spiritual gifts?

Read Ephesians 4:4-6, 11-13.

- What does the character of the Gift Giver tell you about the gifts he gives?

- Why does the Spirit give gifts?

- What does this passage tell you about spiritual gifts?

Get together with your group of four again. Share your answers to the questions above. Then discuss the following questions, and write your answers in the spaces provided.

- How is your group like the body of Christ?

- How would you have felt if some of your group members hadn't shared their information? How is that like Christians who don't use their spiritual gifts?

- Why are spiritual gifts important to the church? to God?

Section 2

Your leader will give you some pieces of candy. You can keep your candy to eat later, or you can earn an equal number of candies by serving others in the room. For example, if you receive two candies, you can earn two more candies by performing two acts of service—tying someone's shoe, for example.

When your group members have finished, discuss these questions and write your answers in the spaces provided.

- Did you keep your candy or earn more? Why?

- What was it like to serve others or be served by others?

- Read Matthew 25:14-30. How is this story like the activity?

- How are spiritual gifts like the talents in the story? How are they different?

- How can spiritual gifts be put to work to produce "more"?

Leader Instructions

After groups have completed the "Grace Gifts" page, process the experience using questions such as these:
- What insights did you gain from this experience?
- What do you think about the role of spiritual gifts in the body of Christ? about your role?

Extension Idea

Consider offering a spiritual-gifts inventory to the students. They could take the inventory before the lesson, or you could present it as an option for those interested in further study. You can find several inventories online by typing in "spiritual gifts" in your search engine, or you can use a printed source such as Network by Bruce Bugbee, Don Cousins, and Bill Hybels.

Apply It

Individually think about which servant in the Matthew Scripture you're most like and why. Then review the list of gifts in the "Read About It" section. Choose one or two gifts you think you might have, then read the passages listed with those gifts. If you still think you might have a gift, circle it.

Write your own brief story about using your gifts. Use these questions to get you started: How could you use your gifts? What "more" could using your gift produce? How would using your gifts affect you? others? the church?

_____

_____

At the top of the gift box below, write your name and any spiritual gifts you circled. Then pass your paper around your small group. As each paper comes to you, do one of the following:

Write about a time you saw this person use one of the gifts.

Write an idea about how this person could use a gift.

Write why this person's gifts are important to the church.

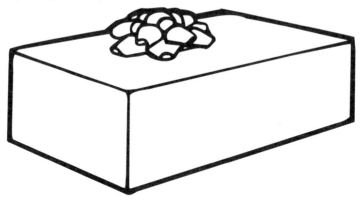

28 ♦ Study 3

When your book returns to you, take a minute to read the comments. Then pray with your group members to thank God for the gifts he has given your group.

Live It

Each day this week, look for one way to use one of your spiritual gifts. If you have the gift of helps, for example, you might volunteer in the church office or do some extra work around your house.

Even if you're unable to use a gift each day, try to implement your gift as you see opportunities. Use the space below to write about your experiences.

_____

_____

Use the space below to describe your ideas for using your gifts in the future.

_____

Tell Me More...

"Don't forget. You are a unique blend of talents, skills, and gifts; you are an indispensable member of the Body of Christ. You can do what only you can do. So don't cheat the rest of us. Get out there and get busy!"

—Charles Stanley, "You Gotta Have Parts,"
Discipleship Journal, Issue Ninety 1995

Tell Me More...

What are the differences between talents and spiritual gifts? While talents and gifts may operate together, there is a difference.

Talents...	Gifts...
are present from physical birth.	are present from spiritual birth.
benefit humanity.	benefit humanity in a spiritual way.
can be used to glorify and benefit many things.	are used to glorify God and bless Christ's body.

Who Am I?

 Our self-esteem comes from God.

Supplies: You'll need Bibles, pens, various craft supplies, modeling clay, markers, and scissors.

Preparation: Set out the supplies on a table.

Leader Instructions

Begin by having students each read the "Read About It" section and respond in the "Write About It" section.

Read About It

I love my two-year-old daughter when she's sleeping. She's quiet and peaceful, and her face is free of the marks of worry. She looks like an angel.

I love her when she's sweet, giving me hugs and kisses and asking me to play with her.

I love her when she entertains me. She runs around and laughs and chases the dog and jumps up and down and claps and cries, "Yea!"

But I also love her when she throws tantrums. She lies on the floor and pounds her fists and screams and kicks. She glares at me in defiance.

I love her when she disobeys, throws her food on the floor, demands candy all day long, refuses to sit in her car seat, takes toys away from other kids, draws on the furniture, and whines.

I may get angry, discipline her, and refuse to grant her requests. But I love her no matter what.

If I, imperfect as I am, can love my daughter all the time, how much more does our perfect God love us, his children? He loves us no matter what.

Write About It

- On a level from one to ten (ten is high), rank your self-esteem right now. Why did you choose that rank?

_____

_____

- What kinds of things can change the way you see yourself?

- Read Genesis 1:27. What does this Scripture tell you about the way God sees you?

Extension Idea

For the Section 1 of the "Beloved Child" activity, you may want to provide clown makeup and have teenagers actually draw faces on each other.

Experience It

Leader Instructions

Have students form four groups, and point out the supply table you prepared before the study.

Follow the instructions on the "Beloved Child" page (p. 32) in your group. Use the supplies on the supply table as needed.

Tell Me More...

There is a positive side to problems with self-esteem. Character is strengthened through adversity. As you face problems and disappointments, you will learn that you are capable of handling them. If you never have to struggle, you may never learn to cope and you won't grow. According to Dr. James Dobson (Focus on the Family, October 1996), we "deserve the right to face problems and profit from the confrontation."

Beloved Child

Section 1

Read Psalm 139:1-6. As a group, discuss the following questions, and write the answers in the spaces provided.

- How would you sum up the meaning of this Scripture in one sentence?

- What does this Scripture tell us about the relationship between God and humans?

Using the art supplies (save the modeling clay for later), take a few minutes to create a face that resembles a "face" people sometimes wear at home, at school, or at church. Then discuss these questions in your group, and write the answers in the spaces provided:

- What different faces do people wear, and why do they wear them?

- What does this Scripture have to say about putting on different faces? How does God see you?

Section 2

Read Psalm 139:7-12. As a group, discuss the following questions and write the answers in the space provided.

- How would you sum up the meaning of this Scripture in one sentence?

- What does this Scripture tell us about the relationship between God and humans?

As a group, list all the places you can think of—anything from "Switzerland" to "my friend John's basement." Now brainstorm for evidence of God's presence in each of those places. Then discuss these questions in your group, and write the answers in the spaces provided.

- Where do you think God's presence is most evident? Why?

- Where do you think God's presence is least evident? Why?

- What does this Scripture say about God's presence?

Section 3

Read Psalm 139:13-16. As a group, discuss the following questions, and write the answers in the spaces provided.

• How would you sum up the meaning of this Scripture in one sentence?

• What does this Scripture tell us about the relationship between God and humans?

Use a piece of modeling clay to create an unusual "invention." When everyone in your group has finished, take turns guessing the name and purpose of each group member's invention. When you're finished, discuss these questions in your group, and write the answers in the spaces provided.

• How did it feel to create something?

• What does this Scripture say about how God may have felt when he created you?

Section 4

Read Psalm 139:17-24. As a group, discuss the following questions, and write the answers in the spaces provided:

• How would you sum up the meaning of this Scripture in one sentence?

• What does this Scripture tell us about the relationship between God and humans?

Form pairs within your group (if you have an uneven number, form one trio and take turns), and have partners stand toe-to-toe. Within each pair, choose one person to be the Mover and one person to be the Mirror. The Mover will make slow motions with his or her face, arms, hands, or torso; the Mirror will attempt to mimic the motions. After about a minute, switch roles. When you're finished, discuss these questions in your group, and write the answers in the spaces provided.

• Was it easy or difficult to mirror someone else's movements? Explain.

• How easy or difficult is it to mirror God and his thoughts? Explain.

• What does this Scripture say about human thoughts and God's thoughts?

Leader Instructions

After groups have finished the "Beloved Child" page, process the experience using questions such as these:

- *What insights have you gained from this experience?*
- *After completing this experience, how do you think God feels about you?*

Apply It

Find a partner, and use a marker to trace your partner's hand on the back of this paper. Then divide the following Scriptures so that each partner will read two of these passages: Romans 8:15-17; Romans 8:38-39; Jeremiah 9:23-24; and Psalm 8. As you read the Scriptures, think about how they show true sources of self-esteem. Afterward, write on the hand that has been traced on your paper how the Scriptures might affect your self-esteem. Then share what you learned with your partner.

Below your partner's hand, write a short prayer thanking God for creating your partner and asking God to help your partner remember the high esteem in which God holds him or her. Afterward, read Romans 5:8 together; then pray your prayers aloud.

Live It

To help build your self-esteem, start by answering the following questions:
- What are your spiritual gifts?

Read Romans 12:6-8 to find out how God wants us to use our gifts. Then look for opportunities to use yours.

- What talents has God given you?

Thank God for blessing you with these abilities and for the privilege of using them for him.

_____

- How would you feel if you gave someone a gift and he or she responded by saying, "It's OK, but it's not as nice as the one you gave my brother"?

That's essentially what we're saying to God when we compare ourselves with others. Whenever you find yourself playing the comparison game, stop and thank God for what you do have instead of dwelling on what you don't have.

_____

- Who are three positive, enthusiastic people you can talk to about the subject of self-image?

Find those people and ask them to help you. If you can't think of anyone, you may want to consider talking to a Christian counselor. Meeting with someone who really knows how to listen and offer wisdom is a great way to receive insight into your self-image.

_____

The Making of a Hero

 **Christ is our one true hero.**

Supplies: You'll need Bibles and pens.

Preparation: Set out the supplies on a table.

Leader Instructions

Begin by having students each read the "Read About It" section and respond in the "Write About It" section.

Read About It

One of Aesop's fables, "The Brave Mice," tells the story of a cat that caught all the mice she could find in the barn.

One day the mice had a meeting to talk about the problem of the cat. The mice proposed several plans for staying away from the dangerous cat.

A very wise, old, gray mouse proposed this solution: that they hang a bell around the cat's neck. Then when they heard the bell ring, they would know the cat was approaching and they could hide.

The other mice agreed that this was a good plan. But when the old, gray mouse asked who would be the one to tie the bell around the cat's neck, everyone refused and ran away to hide.

Write About It

• What makes a hero?

_____
_____
_____

- When have you had the opportunity to be a hero, and how did you respond?

- When have you heard people talk about their heroic character without acting accordingly? When has this been true of you?

- Are Christ's actions similar to the characteristics of a hero? Explain, using examples.

Experience It

Leader Instructions

Have students form groups of four, and point out the supply table you prepared before the study.

Follow the instructions on the "Heroes" page (p. 38) in your group. Use the supplies on the supply table as needed.

Tell Me More...

In 1 Timothy 4:12-16, we find a call to heroism that affects Christ's followers even now. The Apostle Paul encouraged Timothy to uphold his leadership position with courage but without using his youth as an excuse for setbacks. Timothy was urged to be a hero by teaching the gospel as he'd been taught and modeling behavior that would glorify the Lord. He was told that without this kind of heroism, the young Christian faith could die a quick death. Even though Timothy faced struggles within the church and was threatened with danger from outside the church, he met the challenge. Surely we can too.

Heroes
Section 1

In the chart below, write the names of five of your personal heroes (leave the last line blank for now). Then list some of their character traits. Finally, describe some of their actions and indicate whether those actions have been positive or negative.

Name	Character Traits	Actions

When everyone in your group has finished the chart, take turns sharing what you wrote. Then discuss the following questions, and write your thoughts in the spaces provided.

• What about these people make them heroic to you?

• Have your heroes ever done less than heroic things or acted in less than heroic ways? Explain.

In your group, read Hebrews 12:1-3. Then fill in the last line of the chart with Jesus' name, traits, and actions. Afterward, discuss the following questions with your group members, and write your thoughts in the spaces provided.

• What about Jesus makes him heroic?

• How do you decide who your heroes are?

- How can looking up to someone help you succeed or fail?

_____

_____

- What kinds of characteristics and behaviors do you want to emulate? Why?

_____

_____

- What difference would it make in your life if you fixed your eyes on Christ as your one true hero?

_____

_____

Section 2

In your group, take turns reading aloud Hebrews 11. Choose two situations from the many heroic situations mentioned, and discuss the underlying moral issue in each situation. For example, Abraham had to decide whether or not to trust God to lead him to a foreign country. Write the information in the space provided below next to "Moral issue." Then think of a situation from your own life that involves a similar moral issue. For example, maybe you struggled to trust God when you had to go to a new school. Write the information in the space provided below next to "Personal situation."

Next discuss the biblical hero's actions in the situation. Write the information in the space provided next to "Bible hero's behavior."

Then discuss how modern people facing similar moral issues could act as heroically as the biblical people did. Write the information in the space provided next to "Possible modern heroic reaction."

1. Situation from the passage:
   Moral issue: _____
   Bible hero's behavior: _____
   Personal situation: _____
   Possible modern heroic reaction: _____

2. Situation from the passage:
   Moral issue: _____
   Bible hero's behavior: _____
   Personal situation: _____
   Possible modern heroic reaction: _____

Discuss these questions and write your thoughts in the spaces provided.

- Would these biblical figures be considered heroes today? Why or why not?

- What might be difficult about heroically responding to these biblical situations in modern times?

- How can looking to Christ as your one true hero help you to heroically respond to difficult situations?

Leader Instructions

After groups have finished the "Heroes" page, process the experience using questions such as these:

- How does Christ compare to the worldly heroes you thought of in the first section?
- What different heroic responses did you think of in the second section?
- What did you learn about heroism from this experience?

Apply It

In your group, read 1 Timothy 4:12-16. Then discuss these questions, and write your thoughts in the spaces provided.

- Summarize how Paul tells Timothy to be a role model.

_____

_____

- How does this role model reflect Christ's characteristics?

_____

_____

- How is Jesus a role model to you?

_____

_____

Think of a situation you're struggling with right now—a moral dilemma or difficult problem you're facing. For example, maybe a friend is pressuring you to attend a party your parents have forbidden you to attend. In the box below, draw a picture of how you'd handle the situation if you were a hero with the characteristics Paul outlined to Timothy. On your picture, label what makes the hero heroic. For example, draw a line from the hero's mouth and write, "Teaches others to do the right thing."

The Making of a Hero ◆ 41

Share your drawing with your group, discuss these questions, and write your thoughts in the spaces provided.

• How does the hero you drew reflect the fact that Christ is our one true hero?

_____

_____

• What are some benefits of having Christ as our one true hero?

_____

_____

Finally, pray with your group that God will give you the faith and courage to act as Christlike heroes in your own life.

Live It

Think of two people from your church whom you respect. Find their phone numbers in a phone book or church directory. Write their names and phone numbers in the spaces provided. Call the two people and ask them to describe something heroic they've seen or done that glorified God. You may use the following script as a guide:

"Hello, [person's name]. This is [your name] from [name of church group]. We've recently completed a Bible study on heroes. One of our projects is to call church members and ask them about the most heroic things done in the name of Christ that they've witnessed. Can you think of an experience in which you saw or even did something heroic that glorified God? I'd like to share it with our group."

Write their answers in the spaces provided, and share what you discovered at your next meeting.

Name: _____

Phone number: _____

Experience: _____

_____

_____

Name: _____

Phone number: _____

Experience: _____

_____

Tell Me More...

The writer of the book of Hebrews was clearly trying to motivate his audience, which lacked faith and conviction. In chapter 11, the author reminded the people of the heroes of their faith in order to encourage their own heroism in troubled times. In chapter 12, the author rallied the people to throw off those things that held them back and focus on their one true hero, Jesus. With our eyes on Jesus, we gain courage and faith instead of weariness and resignation. With our eyes on Jesus, we, too, can be heroes of the faith as God intends us to be.

Tell Me More...

"The legacy of heroes is the memory of a great name and the inheritance of a great example."

—Benjamin Disraeli, quoted at www.cyber-nation.com/victory/quotations

Extension Idea

Have students sign up to be accountability partners. Have pairs agree to connect with each other regularly over the next month and hold each other accountable as they work to be positive role models that exemplify Christ.

It's Who You Are That Counts

  God wants us to focus on him rather than on being popular.

Supplies: You'll need Bibles, pens, and markers.

Preparation: Set out the supplies on a table.

Leader Instructions

Begin by having students each read the "Read About It" section and respond in the "Write About It" section.

Read About It

What is your price?

What will it take for you to turn away from what you know is true?

For what will you destroy what you know is precious?

Will you rework your beliefs to keep a cute guy or a beautiful girl? Will you refuse to defend another person when someone influential hurts him or her? Will you stop short of doing right simply because it costs you time or money? Will you ridicule rather than meet a need because you don't want to look weak?

For each of us, the selling point is different. But you can keep from selling out simply by giving yourself to God. It's not just a mental thing; it's an action thing. It's called submission.

In submitting to God, you'll gain the sense of acceptance and goodness you used to work for in weaker ways. And God will give you the strength you need to keep from selling out. This is the power of true submission to God—the power to work for all that is good and right and true and Christlike.

Write About It

- How can submission to God keep us from living for popularity?

- What groups or cliques can you identify in your school? How do people in those groups relate to people in other groups?

- If Jesus were to come to your high school, which group(s) do you think he would fit in with? Why?

Extension Idea

Instead of drawing the illustrations for People Illustrated, consider using photos from magazines to create collages.

Experience It

Leader Instructions

Have students form groups of four, and point out the supply table you prepared before the study.

Congratulations! You have been chosen as the editorial and design team for a hot new magazine, People Illustrated. For each spread in the "People Illustrated" insert of this book (pp. 46-48), read the instructions at the top of the page, then work as a team to create the text and accompanying illustrations in the blank section of the page. Use the supplies on the supply table as needed.

People Illustrated

Read 1 Corinthians 3:1-4. Discuss the following questions in your group, then write in the blank area below a paraphrase of these verses that would apply to your school.

- Who are the different people or groups that students tend to follow at your school? (See verse 4.)
- Paul reminded the Corinthians that their leaders were "mere men." What reminder would you give people who follow popular students or try to get into groups they think are cool?
- What kinds of problems do struggles for popularity or power (verse 3) lead to in your school?
- Do you agree that cliques and power struggles are a sign of immaturity? (See verses 1-2.) What advice would you give to yourself or your classmates regarding this issue?

Now write a contemporary version of verses 1-4 in the blank space below.

A picture paints a thousand words—that's why we call this magazine People Illustrated—so create an illustration of the different groups or cliques people might notice when they visit your school.

Read 1 Corinthians 3:5-15. Discuss the following questions in your group, then write in the blank section below a paraphrase of these verses that would apply to your school.

- What does it mean to you that you are God's building or field? (See verse 9.)
- What do you think it means to be careful how we build? (See verse 10.)
- What is more important in God's eyes than what group we are in or how popular we are?

Now write your own version of verses 5-15 in the blank space below.

In your group, come up with a visual idea of what your school would look like if every Christian concentrated on growing in Christ (like God's field) or helping build one another up instead of concentrating on status. Use the space below for your illustration.

Read 1 Corinthians 3:16-17. Discuss the following questions in your group, then write in the blank section a paraphrase of these verses that would apply to your school.
- What are some ways that people harm their bodies for the sake of popularity?
- What does the fact that God chose your body to live in tell you about how he values you? How does that compare or contrast with what society values in body image?

Now write your own version of verses 16-17 in the blank space below.

Take your pick for this page: You can either illustrate the damaging things people do in their quest to be cool, or you can illustrate what it means to you that God lives in you.

It's Who You Are That Counts ♦ 47

Read 1 Corinthians 3:18-23. Discuss the following questions in your group, then write in the blank section a paraphrase of these verses that would apply to your school.

- What are some things that are cool "by the standards of this age"? (See verse 18.)
- How do those things compare or contrast with what is cool by God's standards?
- How can social status be deceptive? (See verse 18.)
- Carefully read verses 21-23. Do you think God promises that you can be in any social group you want if you focus first on God? Why or why not? What do you think Paul means when he says, "All things are yours"?
- What would it take for you to give up concentrating on being popular and concentrate on being the person God wants you to be?

Now write your own version of verses 18-23 in the blank space below.

Make this page a personal illustration. Depict yourself as the kind of person God wants you to be when you relate to others. Maybe it means reaching out to people you think are less popular than you are. Maybe it means finding the good in people you resent because they think they are cooler than you. Either way, it means "you are of Christ" (verse 23).

Leader Instructions

After groups have finished the "People Illustrated" section, process the experience using questions such as these:

- Do you think it's wrong to be popular? Explain.
- What could be some dangers in popularity? How could you use popularity for God?
- Do you think it's wrong to have a group of friends with whom you hang out regularly? Explain.
- What could be some dangers in sticking with a close group of friends? How could God use your group of friends?
- What in 1 Corinthians 3 was the most encouraging for you?
- What in 1 Corinthians 3 was the most challenging for you?

Apply It

Find a partner, preferably someone you know fairly well. Trade books with your partner, and use the "Personal Letter" page (p. 50) to write your own letter encouraging and challenging your partner. You can use the outline to model your letter after Paul's letter in 1 Corinthians 3, or you can write your own letter.

When you're finished, read the letter to your partner, then return the book to your partner.

Tell Me More...

Even in grade school, Steven Curtis Chapman faced a dilemma: to be popular by the "in" crowd's terms or to be popular on his own terms. Steven's faith was important to him, and he didn't want to compromise it.

At the same time, he just wanted to be everyone's friend. "I wanted to get along with everybody," Steven...explains now. So he decided to live what he believed and hope people would like him anyway...

He continued to be himself and pursue interests even if they were "unpopular." He tried to be the best Christian he could be, and he treated people the same—no matter what clique they were in.

By the end of his high school years, people recognized what Steven had done. Steven's classmates voted to give him the highest honors possible at Heath High School, naming him "Mr. Heath" and "Mr. Senior"...

Steven had proven that it's not whom you know but who you are that matters most of all.

(*The Youth Bible,* Word Publishing)

Personal Letter

Dear   ,

It can seem so important to fit in with the cool crowd. Sometimes I feel…

_____
_____
_____
_____

But I want you to remember that having a Christlike character is what really counts. I see God growing and building this character in you in these ways:

_____
_____
_____
_____

Whenever you feel pressure to compromise because of what some group seems to expect of you, please remember…

_____
_____
_____
_____

I want to challenge you to see yourself as…

_____
_____
_____

and to respond to others by…

_____
_____
_____
_____

Sincerely,

Live It

This week reflect on the issue of popularity in light of Jesus' experience. Read Isaiah 53:2-3.

- Based on this description of Jesus, how popular do you think he would be in your school?

  _____
  _____

- Name one person in your school who you prefer not to be seen with because that person would lower your social standing. Be honest; no one will see this but you.

  _____
  _____

- Now imagine treating that person the way you would treat Jesus. What would you do?

  _____
  _____

- Maybe you feel as if you are the unpopular one at school. How does it make you feel to know that Jesus was physically unattractive and rejected?

  _____
  _____

- Think of the "cool" people who tend to intimidate you. Write their names here. Don't worry; this is private.

  _____
  _____

- How would Jesus treat these people?

  _____
  _____

Do you want to have Christlike character? Choose to treat the people "above" and "below" you on the social ladder the way you would treat Christ and the way Christ would treat them. It takes guts. It's risky. But it's worth it!

True Success

 True success comes from surrendering our lives to God.

Supplies: You'll need Bibles and pens.

Preparation: Set out the supplies on a table.

Leader Instructions

Begin by having students each read the "Read About It" section and respond in the "Write About It" section.

Read About It

By her twenty-first birthday, Henrietta Howland Robinson Green was worth more than five million dollars—and that was back when five million dollars could buy a few things. Like an entire country.

Hetty's grandfather had explained to her early on what could be accomplished on the stock market, and Hetty was a good student…When she died, she left an estate estimated at one hundred million dollars.

She is remembered by some as the "witch of Wall Street." She was such a penny-pincher that she even neglected treating her son's medical condition for so long that eventually he had to have a leg amputated…

Hetty is listed in the *Guinness Book of World Records* not as the richest woman in the world. Not as the happiest. Not as the most generous. She's listed as the "Most Miserly Woman in the World."

(Les Christie, in *Five-Star Stories From All-Star Youth Leaders*)

Write About It

- In what ways was Henrietta Howland Robinson Green successful in life? Why was she successful?

- In what ways was Henrietta a failure in life? Why?

- Using the same criterion you used to judge Henrietta, how successful are you in life? What measures do you use to define success?

- Read Matthew 19:16-21. Henrietta had been told how to grow up by her grandfather. He showed her how to work the stock market. But what if Henrietta had been presented with Jesus' words? How might her life have been different? What does this passage say to you about Jesus' definition of a successful life?

Experience It

> ### Leader Instructions
>
> Have students form groups of three, and point out the supply table you prepared before the study.
>
> Ask half the trios each to prepare a thirty-second radio commercial about how money provides security. Ask the other half each to prepare a thirty-second radio commercial about how money gives people significance. After students have worked for five minutes, call trios together to perform their commercials.
>
> When all the trios have performed, give them another five minutes to work. This time ask half the trios each to create a thirty-second commercial about how God provides security, and ask the other half each to create a thirty-second commercial about how God gives people significance. Then call trios together again to perform their new commercials. After the performances, have the entire group discuss these questions:
> - Which commercials were particularly convincing? Why?
> - What reasons surfaced most often for why money makes people successful?
> - What reasons surfaced most often for why knowing God makes people successful?
>
> Have trios gather again.

Follow the instructions on the "What's Success?" page (p. 54) in your group. Use the supplies on the supply table as needed.

What's Success?

To feel that your life is successful, how much of the following resources would you need? Work independently to fill out the survey below. When you're finished, share your answers with your trio members.

Success Survey

Your name: _____

Date: _____

To consider myself successful, I would need the following amounts of these resources:

Money: _____ dollars

Daily free time: _____ hours

Education: _____ degree completed

Possessions: _____

_____

Recognition: (What accomplishment would signal your success to yourself and the people you love?):

_____

In your trio, read aloud Matthew 19:16-30, discuss the following questions, and write your answers in the spaces provided.

- How sincere was the young man in wanting to improve morally? Why did you answer as you did?

_____

_____

- What, in your own words, was the choice Jesus gave the young man?

_____

_____

- What would the world have thought of the young man's success if he'd followed Jesus? What would God have thought?

_____

_____

- If you were to ask Jesus what you still lack to be perfect, what would Jesus tell you to do? (The survey you filled out earlier may help you decide.)

_____

_____

- Would you do what he asked? Why or why not?

_____

_____

Apply It

In your trio, sit knee to knee—as close as possible. Before continuing, agree that nothing you share in your small group will leave your group. You'll keep quiet about what you hear—no exceptions, unless there's a legal obligation to go to the police.

On the one-dollar bill below, write the days of the week.

Then discuss these questions in your trio:
- How are you like or unlike the rich young man who talked with Jesus?
- What, if anything, is keeping you from following Jesus wholeheartedly?
- Why haven't you dealt with it in the past?
- What could you do to deal with it now?

Decide what's most important to you: success in the eyes of your world or success in the eyes of God. Do you most want the kingdom of God or the kingdom you see now?

On the one-dollar bill above, write an idea for every day of the week to encourage yourself to turn toward Christ and away from the things that stand between you and Christ. Brainstorm with your group members for ideas. Then agree to pray for each other throughout the week—and beyond.

Begin now. Pray to God for help in making changes and growing closer to him. Pledge to God your willingness to change.

A song that does a great job contrasting the difference between success in the world and success in the kingdom of God is "Only a Fool" by Geoff Moore and the Distance.

Listen to the song and consider these questions:
- *Who are the fools in this song? Why?*
- *Who does this song bring to your mind? Why?*
- *If the author included a verse about you, what would you want it to say?*

True Success ♦ 55

Live It

This week, refer often to the commitments you wrote in the "Apply It" section. Every day, jot a few words on the bill above that summarize how you're facing the issue you've described. Over the course of seven days, watch what God is doing in your life.

Tell Me More...

Has Jesus got something against rich people?

That's the message sometimes pulled from Matthew 19:16-30—that being rich means you've failed spiritually and that living correctly means you'd give everything away, always.

Umm...no.

It *is* harder for rich people to enter heaven, but not simply because they're rich. If that were true, Jesus would have told *everybody* to ditch their belongings. Jesus was speaking specifically to the young man questioning him, but there's a message for us, too. Anything standing in the way of our wholehearted devotion to Christ is like this young man's riches. That's what we need to get rid of.

Tell Me More...

There's a danger when people seek "success" in life.

For starters, Jesus never suggested that success (as most people define it) is a goal worth pursuing. In the kingdom of God the first are last, the last are first, and children are examples of a trusting faith that pleases God. Being successful isn't a matter of money. Or credentials. Or even good deeds.

Success comes with faithfulness and obedience—hardly the stuff that gets you a guest shot on *The Tonight Show*.

Here's the rub: Everyone applauds talent, but in the end it's integrity that pays off. God's "well done" is reserved for servants who are *faithful*.

One Step at a Time

 We can trust God to guide our future.

Supplies: You'll need Bibles, pens, and three strips of cloth (about four inches wide and twelve inches long) for every four people.

Preparation: Set out the supplies on a table.

Begin by having students each read the "Read About It" section and respond in the "Write About It" section.

Read About It

"Your word is a lamp to my feet and a light for my path."

—Psalm 119:105

Abby walked hesitantly along the path through the woods. She hadn't known the night could be so dark. The moon was hidden behind the clouds, and the stars seemed tired and dim.

As she walked, the light of her lantern swung back and forth on the ground. She held it up and squinted at the darkness. She could manage to see only what the lantern illuminated for her—a few feet in front of her.

She felt a sudden twinge of fear. She didn't know what was beyond that lantern light, and if she allowed her fear to overwhelm her...

She took a deep breath and let it out, watching it cloud up in front of her face. She would take her journey one step at a time, walking in the light of her lantern.

Write About It

- What questions about your future would you like to ask God?

_____

_____

Extension Idea

Consider playing a recording of the song "Thy Word" as students reflect on Psalm 119:105.

- What do you think about the interpretation of Psalm 119:105 in the quote on page 57? Why do you think God would choose to reveal our future paths only a step at a time?

___

- Have you experienced God's guidance in your life? If so, how?

___

Experience It

Leader Instructions

Have students form groups of four, and point out the supply table you prepared before the study.

You are about to embark on a journey to explore the relationship between God's guidance and an individual's future. This journey is represented by Joseph's journey in the Bible. As you travel, you will retrace the steps that Joseph took from his father's fields to Pharaoh's palace. At each "stop," you will find instructions about what to read and what to record in your log book (pp. 60-62). Happy traveling!

Tell Me More...

When Jeremiah spoke these words of hope—" 'For I know the plans I have for you,' declares the Lord, 'plans to prosper you and not to harm you, plans to give you hope and a future' " (Jeremiah 29:11)—he was speaking to Israelites who had been overpowered and carried away as prisoners of war to Babylon. Imagine how difficult it must have been to believe in any kind of a future! Yet God was faithful to his promise; the Israelites began returning to Jerusalem from Babylon in 538 B.C.

Time Line of Joseph's Journey

- **The Fields**
  - Joseph's jealous brothers sell him into slavery.

- **Potiphar's House**
  - Joseph becomes the top servant to one of Pharaoh's officials.

- **The Prison**
  - Potiphar's wife, angry because she can't seduce Joseph, has him thrown into prison.
  - While there, Joseph interprets the dream of two of Pharaoh's imprisoned servants: the baker and the cupbearer.

- **The Palace**
  - Joseph's interpretations of the servants' dreams prove correct, but the cupbearer forgets all about Joseph. (The baker gets beheaded, so he's not much help either.)
  - When Pharaoh has troubling dreams, the cupbearer remembered and recommends Joseph.
  - Joseph warns Pharaoh of a coming famine and outlines a plan to prepare for it.
  - Pharaoh makes Joseph second-in-command over all Egypt.
  - Ultimately Joseph's work saves not only Egypt during the famine, but his own family (who are, incidentally, God's chosen people).

Tell Me More...

Although Joseph and his brothers didn't realize it at first, Joseph was to play a key role in the history of God's people. Speaking to his brothers, Joseph summarized everything that had happened this way: "You intended to harm me, but God intended it for good to accomplish what is now being done, the saving of many lives" (Genesis 50:20). Not coincidentally, among those many lives saved were those of the ancestors of Jesus Christ.

Log Book

Stop 1: The Fields

Look at a copy of "Joseph's Journey" on page 59. One person in your group should read aloud the "Tell Me More…" box; another person should read aloud Genesis 37:12-28. Make the following entries in your log book based on the group's conclusions.

- Entry 1: On a scale of one to ten, how much in control of his future do you think Joseph felt?

- Entry 2: What events or actions show us, as readers who know the plans God had for Joseph, that God was in control of Joseph's future?

- Entry 3: Has anyone in the group had an experience in which they felt abandoned by God, and later realized God had been active all along? Record this experience in the log book.

Stop 2: Potiphar's House

Have someone read aloud Genesis 39:1-6a. Make the following entries based on your group's conclusions.

- Entry 1: List three pairs of adjectives or phrases that contrast Joseph's situation at the last stop with Joseph's situation in Potiphar's house—for example, "hit bottom vs. upwardly mobile."

- Entry 2: What evidence do you see of God's involvement in Joseph's current situation? (Notice what the passage tells us directly, but also think about the implications of Joseph's being in the household of a leading official.)

- Entry 3: Notice that throughout his "journey," Joseph is given important responsibilities (see Genesis 39:4, 6, 22-23; 41:41). Write a statement that summarizes how your group sees the role of individual responsibility within the framework of God's larger plan for the future.

- Entry 4: Reread Genesis 39:3. What role do you think God plays in your successes? How do you feel about giving God credit for what you achieve?

Stop 3: The Prison

Have someone read aloud Genesis 39:6b-18. Make the following entries based on your group's conclusions.

- Entry 1: How does Joseph's response to Potiphar's wife influence his future?

- Entry 2: Does Joseph's response to Potiphar's wife reflect Joseph's character or God's plan for Joseph's future?

- Entry 3: What do you think is the relationship between our character and God's plan for our future?

- Entry 4: If God was in control of Joseph's future, how do you explain the fact that Joseph had to face this temptation?

Tell Me More...

To further explore the issue of temptation and God's plan for our future, read aloud James 1:13-14 and 1 Corinthians 10:13. Based on those verses, which statement(s) best describe how God guides us?

- God permits us to be tempted.
- God causes us to be tempted.
- God protects us from temptation by making it impossible for us to give in.
- God protects us from temptation by making it possible for us not to give in.

Have someone read aloud Genesis 39:19-23.

- Entry 5: What evidence do you have that even in this situation God has a plan for Joseph's future?

Stop 4: The Palace

Have someone read aloud Genesis 41:33-43.

From the supply table, take three pieces of cloth for your group. Label one "God's Plan for the Future." On that piece, record events that show that God was influencing Joseph's life. Label a second piece of cloth "Joseph's Choices." On that cloth, record the actions that Joseph took. Now braid the two strands together with the third piece of cloth.

- Entry 1: How does your braided strand illustrate the relationship between God's control and human responsibility?

- Entry 2: How have you seen that interconnection in your own life? Record responses from several people in the group.

- Entry 3: Have each person contribute one word that describes how he or she feels about God's involvement in his or her future. Write those words here.

Leader Instructions

Bring the groups back together, and process the experience with questions such as these:

- How far into his future do you think Joseph could see at any point in his journey? How does this relate to the idea that God gives light for just the next step (as suggested in the "Read About It" section)?
- How do you think Joseph's experiences affected his faith? Explain.
- What was the relationship between Joseph's character and the way God directed his future? What are the implications of that for you?
- Read Jeremiah 29:11. How was this passage true for Joseph? How is it true for you?

Apply It

On your own, read Romans 8:28-39. Draw your own time line in the space that follows, indicating times you were "in the pits" like Joseph, times things were going well for you, and times you felt you couldn't see very far ahead.

Now find a partner and share your time line with each other. Then discuss these questions:

- What does Romans 8:28-39 tell you about your future?

- How have you seen God working for your good in a difficult situation?

Extension Idea

You may wish to have groups actually move from one designated spot to another as they discuss the "stops" on Joseph's journey.

- How does that experience influence your faith? your character?

Live It

This week reflect on 1 Thessalonians 4:13-5:11 as you think about your future. Read the passage, and answer the following questions:

- Do you personally believe that Jesus died and rose again? (See 1 Thessalonians 4:14; 5:10.) If so, how does that give you confidence in your future? If not, think of someone you could talk with about your doubts, and set up an appointment this week.

- How can knowing God's plan for the end of time give you hope for the present?

- How can you encourage others (1 Thessalonians 4:18; 5:11) about their future?

- What does this passage teach you about the kind of character you should develop as you anticipate the future God has for you? Carefully read 1 Thessalonians 5:6-8, and list character qualities below.

- How well do those qualities describe you? Circle a character trait that you especially want to develop in yourself. Ask God every day to help you grow in that area.